Naomi Foyle

The World Cup

First published in 2010
by Waterloo Press (Hove)
95 Wick Hall
Furze Hill
Hove BN3 1PF

Printed in Palatino 10.7pt by
One Digital
54 Hollingdean Road
East Sussex BN2 4AA

Cover photo © John Luke Chapman 2010
Author photo © Paul van Gelder 2010
Cover design © Waterloo Press 2010

Naomi Foyle is hereby identified as author of this
work in accordance with Section 77 of the Copyright,
Designs and Patents Act 1988

A CIP record for this book is available
from the British Library

ISBN 978-1-906742-21-8

By the same author

The Night Pavilion (Waterloo Press, 2008)
Grace of the Gamblers: A Chantilly Chantey
(Waterloo Press, 2009)
Canada (Echo Room Press, 2005)
Red Hot & Bothered (Lansdowne Press, 2003)
Febrifugue (Treeplantsink Press, 1996)
Hush: An Opera In Two Bestial Acts
(Theatre Passe Muraille, Toronto, 1990)

Acknowledgements

Thanks are due to the editors of the following publications:

Agenda Online, Ambit, Coasters, Commonhead, Fortnight (Belfast), *The London Magazine, Nineties Poetry, Orbis, Oriel, Poet Mountain* (Seoul), *Poetry London, Poetry Wales, the Recusant, Red Hot & Bothered* (Lansdowne Press), *Red Poets, The Rialto, The Slab,* www.transcend.org, www.3cworldfiction.com (Japan).

'The Holiday' was long-listed for The Bridport Prize, 2006.

An AHRC doctoral award provided time to write some of these poems, under the rigorous yet sensitive supervision of Carol Rumens.

Rowyda Amin, James Burt, Hugh Dunkerley, Niall McDevitt, Kai Merriott, John O'Donoghue, Bethan Roberts, David Swann and Lorna Thorpe were insightful early readers of these poems. The editorial acumen of Alan Morrison and Simon Jenner improved the book immensely. Matilda Persson went the extra mile in her design of book and cover. John Luke Chapman developed my original vision for the cover image with his usual unusual flair. Catherine Lupton, in a light-drenched moment on the South Downs, gifted me with the title.

My profound thanks and admiration go to everyone who is working to end the brutal and illegal Israeli occupation of Palestine. I am especially grateful to Elle Osborne and the Violin4Gaza donators, who gave me such a particular sense of purpose and community on the Gaza Freedom March; to Smash EDO Decommissioner Elijah Smith for his letters; and Rowyda Amin for the Arabic lessons and many discussions about political poetry.

And finally, a kiss to Paul van Gelder, companion on many essential journeys.

Contents

Postcard Sent By Someone Else 17
The Church 18
A Long-Eared Tall Tale 20
A *Chupacabra*'s Memory of Fruit 21
Sisters of Mercy 22
Poem for a Greek Anarchist 27
The Red Devil 28
Wake Turbulence 30
Brenda and Isabelle's Place 31
Lean Streets 33
Ground Zero 35
Childless 36
Route 24 38
[and 13 Israelis] 39
Not A/Haibun 40
Open Poem to Fred Voss 43
How it happens here 46
We Are Coming To Gaza 50
Rhetorical Devices 52
God Save Our Noble Team 53
The Turning Point 56
Teutonic Shifts 57
Ancient History 58
Musée de Moyan Âge 59
English Eccentrics in Love 60
Late Works 62
Sefton Park 64
Shape Maven 67
The Coastal Path 68
Swimming at Land's End 70
The Jellyfish 71
The Nude Beach 72
Unlucky Stars 74
Sitting In the Window of Al Casbah Restaurant 76
The London *Fleadh* 77
The Find 78
Secretary to the Sea 79
The Arsonist 80
The Pablo Neruda Barbeque 81

Brighton Beach   82
The Undertow   83
Peter Crouch   84
Skin-Dipped   86
Plaka   87
The Holiday   88
You Never Say Goodbye to a Myth   89
The Minotaur   90
In the Lap of The Gods   91
Merry Crisis   92
What's Jung Got To Do With It?   96
In The Square   97
Purge-aholics   98
The Lammas Rug   99
The Last Phone Call   100
Lilith Remembers the Good Times   102
Resurrection   103
The Cruyff Turn   104
Graham's Ninetieth Birthday   106
Fantasy Football   107
Plaka (ps)   108

Notes

for Wendy Phillips
Bud of Buds

Time lacks experience. Therefore I am not quite
Confounded by history,
Being of the hopeful race of the earth,
Promised to promise, a mystery to mystery,
By which I am not altogether mystified …

Muriel Spark, 'Canaan'

Sometimes you get submerged by emotion. I think it's very
important to express it — which doesn't necessarily mean hitting
someone.

Eric Cantona

The World Cup

Postcard Sent By Someone Else

I would have called last week, but
there was a riot at a football game, the police
shot a woman and her child, then the crowd
set fire to the post office and ripped
all the phones in the *zocalo*
out of their sockets ...

I would have told you that this jungle
is the maw of the world—its hot breath
steams you open in your sleep, then, like
a trickle of army ants dismantling a palm tree,
a screech of howler monkeys shaking
the afternoon rains from the canopy
above your *hamaca*,
                       its enzymes
start breaking you down ...

'THE CHURCH, against drugs, sects and neo-indigenism'
La Journada, May 11th, 1996. Chiapas, Mexico.

For two days they occupied Cathedral Plaza
   with their plastic sheets
     and fire pits,
   their bags of beans,
     rice and corn,
  hot off the loom of the soil.

With pointed demands they constructed a stage
   for their loudspeakers,
     their amplified Tzotzil
         and music

    contra *el terrorismo*
    in the breeze.

These times are not a dance floor,
   but deep into the night,
     with notable reserve,
       the men in their straw hats
        moved brusquely,
   with intimate formality,
to the electric sounds
   of ancient colours —
     the turquoise sizzle
      and burnt sienna pulse
       of the earth beneath us all.

Elaine and I found ourselves
  at a respectful distance
surrounded by the brilliant eyes
  and diamond designs
  of the village sisters —
     young girls giggling
      at our awe?
Perhaps, but their flashing glances
   were not impolite.

Suddenly, with a serious welcome,
  a grandmother
      took us by the hands

'We are here because we are suffering,'
  she said, her gold tooth glinting
like the spark of a sixth sun,
  'Are you ladies more than tourists?'

'*Si, si.*' If at all possible, yes.

I thought I had now become a witness,
  would tell the English-speaking world
'Who-peace-bah' *y 'hermosa'* and 'beautiful'
    without question, *sin egal*.

  Elaine returned
 with food and blankets
in the open tomorrow
   of her warmth.

And for two days in San Cristobal
      trees grew
      in the little mountains
   between sleeping babies and their liberty.

Yes, when the 'neo-indigenous' came to the Plaza
    they brought and left their own earth.

And for two days after the disappearance
    of their sturdy bodies,
  the incense of their sweat
    clung around the church.

A Long-Eared Tall Tale

I was finally on my way to get married (and not just to stay in the country), when the bus to my fiancé's *pueblo* was attacked by thirteen undernourished but still highly effective *chupacabras*. In the gruelish pre-dawn it seemed there might be some truth to the popular conjecture that the creatures are the result of an unholy mating of giant vampire bat, jaguar and howling monkey. There was little time, however, to contemplate their pinprick eyes, Klaus Kinski ears, and long sparse mottled fur. In less than a minute they drained my *novio* of all his blood. And when I whipped out my drawing pad to try and trace some evidence of our hitherto un-witnessed assailants— or at least make a note of his final gurgles for his loved ones—the *chupacabras* separated me from their horde of victims and carried me off to their lair.

High up in a *cieba* tree, I was kept alive on a diet of warm gringa plasma, and instructed to paint the *chupacabras*' portraits in a sensitive light. They are naturally shy and don't trust *periodistas* one drop. ('Jealous of our efficiency' was their verdict, as I came to understand the Morse code clickings of their black and pointed tongues.) Indeed, they were hurt by the various media caricatures of their presumed appearance, and directed me to capture a certain gentleness I had to admit did flit about their features after a particularly sumptuous feed, or a refreshing upside-down nap. I was always treated with the greatest of care, and in my three month detainment was not once molested. *Chupacabras* have quite enough going on in their gene pool without adding an inherited predilection for polished cutlery to the mix, thank you very much.

After I completed the thirteenth drawing, all my efforts were destroyed in ceremonial fashion—torn to shreds, masticated, and buried in the muddy bottom of a small, derelict *cenote*. I was then blindfolded, led back to the road, and set free on condition that I never attempted to reduplicate the images I'd made.

But translations of their songs are quite a different tail.

A *Chupacabra*'s Memory of Fruit

Bring your face close to the crown of my skull...
                         Does it not smell ripe?

But I am famished by the sun
                         & your beauty casts no shade.

Now my bones vie for distinction with your veins
& ignited by my adoration of your mouth
     our quiet hunt begins.
                         Our subtle pageantry of stealth

But be careful for there is not time enough for old deceptions
and the scarcest sliver of the truth will travel further than you
think. Be wary, no-one is prepared to surrender everything.
     You must appraise the value of your hearth against
                    the insistence of your pulse.

Take heed, though you savage all my notebooks, you don't know
where I have been. Be warned—to denude the shorelines
          of my smile, your heart will tear across the waves...

with or without the sweet high contemplation of your love.

It seems I am no stranger. In this soft, indulgent land
my every yawn is law, semi-conscious laughter the fruition
of our days. No-one has ever lost a friend like me before.
     Blunder at your risk. Think twice. I have returned
          for your existence. I am not guessing here.

                         Slowly you mature.

Unforeseeable butterflies alight upon our bodies,
                         partake of our extremes.

Their touch outstrips the unevasive pleasures that you seek

Sisters of Mercy

*

swinging
high   above

the
river
Pampanadi

trailing   a carpet
dust   of candles,
& sweat   Om batiks

frayed roots,   a giant
swollen   mango
fruit   tree

our toes
dabbled
in the sunset

ploughed   darkness
the evening   brought
heat   relief

so it was,
on the way
to Goa

we came
to rest,
Naomi & Noa

Noa.
Her soft crew cut
murmured, not of war,
but Buddhist *gompas*, convents,
the source of my long journey
in the mountains.

Hatless nuns
on a blazing plain,
we sought shelter
in empty Elephant Stables,
a dead Queen's bathing pool,
the milk and chrysanthemum anthems
veiling the archways of Hampi Bazaar.

Skin soothed, I turned back toward the sun,
but she led me to a wonder I only half-remember:
in the dim, cool heart of Pampapati Temple,
whose were the upside-down shadows

dancing lightly through a pin-hole

& briefly blotting out the writing on the wall?

& if, in a vision   Saint Leonard had seen us
prostrate in the searing shade   dirt, sweat & hornets
consuming our young flesh

as sticky fingers pressed
PLAY   PAUSE   REWIND
PLAY   PAUSE   REWIND

until *The Sisters of Mercy*
was wrapped round our brains
like a *sari* in flames
he would have arisen   in his Cali Zen cell
stepped naked   as a newborn thought   from a whirlpool
of black tatters   into a silk Armani suit

and like a fiddler soaring   from a warm tin roof
waltzed
out of his window   down over LA

dark hills   moony smog   shattered glitter
Tinsel Town hustlers   wrecked rollerbladers
sleep-famished migrants   Venice Beach Hitlers

until his bare soles
kissed
the cool skin of the sea

& then, the dawn
his foresworn crown of glory
the surf whispering his new name

G-d's groom would have tread
the night's numinous path
to his brides —

O, our *Noa Nao Ba'al*

*

& how did he do it, walk upon the water
            across the black Pacific to the Ocean of India,
      skirting the Tamils' green tear
                  & parting the lips of the river
            destined to become Pampanadi?
   was he light as a lotus?
            did he glide like Michael Jackson?
                        tiptoe blue as Krishna?
   did the Star of David sigh a silver thread of breath
                  he slung around his waist?
or was he not weightless at all?
            did a thousand atmospheres of pressure
      well up into his flesh
                  so he surged, a marble forelock
         of the crashing, cresting stallion
               that churns the cold depths
                        of the world?

   ... and the singing gold rings
            he spun round our knuckles
                  as he knelt on the rocks at our feet?
      were they chiming on the fountain
                  of a whale spout when he found them?
         skimming on the phosphor of a Pilipino harbour?
         falling from the finger stumps
               of a burnt, dismembered goddess?
         or winking in the grins
                  of two adolescent dolphins,
            gifted by a drowning couple
               they'd chivvied
                  back to shore?

*

Noa, with your galaxy of freckles,
  singed smile, bashful lashes,
    your long body, solid as sandstone
      from those two IDF years

        you didn't want to discuss. Noa,
          with your Parisian ex-girlfriend
            & her three crazy cats
              you were hopelessly wandering back to —

            Noa, with your fuzzy Velcro sandals,
              tired heart, why didn't I lean over,
                plant the gentlest of *mezuzahs*
                  on the peeling threshold of your lips?

Poem for a Greek Anarchist

So, Yannis. Democracy is a joke
unworthy of your swift laughter. Peace
is a euphemism for lobotomising the First World
and starving the Third. Arthritis
is a degenerative disease
my mother tells me strikes young people
too stubborn for their years. Patience
is the most infuriating quality
of 'grounded' men,
and when we eat in your Dad's pizzeria,
my facial muscles feel compelled
to comment on your every move.

The sound your swollen finger makes
plucking at the mouth
of the soda bottle
gives my cheekbones definition.
Your saliva falls
in a long slow arc to the patio
like an egg
cracked open by a skyscraper chef
hitting the fry pan
without breaking its yolk
— and my jaw follows
with its own moist curve.

And if my brow gathers
when you stroke
those pomegranate lips with your collar,
it's not because I'm plotting
to overthrow the State. No,
I'm only involved with that soft cotton,
echoing its furrows
above the night vision eyes of 'Naomi the Cat' —
eyes that look at your lap
and see a bomb
in my bed.

The Red Devil

The bartender had *heard* of mineral water;
a request for juice produced
a fizzy, neon syrup
I'm allergic to. So I flaunted my true colours,

ordered a pint from the tap,
while the folk singer stopped strumming
to ¡*Hola!* me, convinced
I was a Basque separatist on tour.

A woman asked if I was Jewish
or an Arab, while in the Gents,
someone (wise, perhaps, to my sobriety)
informed Mairtín I was a cop.

But I was none of the above.
Or all of them at once. A spy from another struggle,
to find a place where I belong,
to feel at home in my own itchy skin.

Finally, beneath a faded Man United flag,
Little Frankie, with his piercings and lisp,
wiggled his bottom, a minnow in denim,
and hugged me like one of his own.

Too small and sharp to eat, Frankie
was as fun as any Brighton queen
until he whispered *he* supported the Provos,
but his friends were 'all for the Real IRA'.

I sat down, shut up, for a *fleadh* you couldn't pay to see:
chummy singalongs — *This Land is My Land*,
and wistful Irish ballads sung by beefy men
who might've planted Semtex in the garden;

a heartfelt homage to the Turkish hunger strikers
'and our own' — the litany
of Catholic dead
lost in an onrush of applause, then

topped off by a chorus of footie anthems
conducted by the Jolly Green Giant:
the entire bar exploding into
'Fuck the Queen and the UDA',

a forest of muscle punching the air,
shooting up from the fractured bedrock
of centuries of fighting
for what may never be.

Wake Turbulence

The zeitgeist delivers another slam dunk:
blows a Boeing out of the sky, sucker punching
hope with an accidental bombing of Queens
the day I fly into New York.

Nervously smiling at strangers, I vie
for an on-board phone: only five lines open
to the space junk hive
we're now aimlessly droning in tune with.

Just two months ago, a gleaming colossus
crumpled at the knees. The commentators
squawked 'Extraordinary!'
                    And today, in Afghanistan,

generals and journalists beam
maps and statistics up to a metal moon;
American planes drop daisy cutters
on the nodding heads of babies and old men;

while high in the mountains, women crouch,
swathed in blue burkas, not knowing
if war will make public their beauty,
or bury their children in snow.

This vulnerable feeling, strapped inside
a tin whistle in the sky. This cramped anxiety,
the prospect of hours before seeing my friends.
The relief, the cheers when Newark Airport reopens —

these emotions are forged stamps in my passport:
just blurred ink mementoes
of the hyped-up half-hour
I skirmished the airspace of terror.

Brenda and Isabelle's Place

Roller blades, yoga mats,
Japanese cartoons, a turquoise iMac,
scented candles, photos of friends.

Indian gauze draped over the bookshelves,
a view of the Natural History Museum,
and its bald marble eye, the new Planetarium;

oatmeal for breakfast, avocado for lunch,
twenty types of herbal tea:
I'm in a safe place, I can breathe.

Here we can hug and kiss
and scream with delight.
Here Isabelle can grow and learn.

Here the godfather sends black duvets and birthday roses,
and Brenda and I can nibble on olives,
talk back to the box:

tell Tony Blair to get a job,
urge Bush to say 'I am dyslexic',
and if Barry Manilow

singing 'Looks Like We Made It'
surrounded by mothers and babies
on *America Today*

brings a unwanted lump to my throat —
I will be teased only once, then forgiven
coz, 'Forget it! That's what Barry Manilow *does*.'

Here 'Please!' means 'Forget it!'
and 'Forget it!' means 'I'm *totally* with you all the way'.
Here is where Brenda lives

with her boots that take no prisoners
her eyes like doll's house china, hands
like lotuses, opening and closing

softly putting things in bowls. And here,
too, lives her daughter, the child who laughs at Chekhov
ju-jitsus the news. She's a lightening rod for joy,

an express train to the point.
They've made this apartment the home of poets
and peace warriors, yoginis of everyday life.

Lean Streets

Out in Brooklyn, tomorrow's famous artists
are fucking with each other's heads, while Soho,
in a freshly-washed window display
of fleshy aggression and lingerie,
is squeezing the galleries way out to Chelsea,
where six figure sums can still be exchanged
for blue felt puppets, walls of rusted steel
and neon violins.

Greenwich Avenue: a twanging arrow
shot from the heart of the Sixties,
slicing through juice bars and palmists,
vintage dresses and inner meridians,
to hit the pinprick bull's eye
of Washington Square Park,
where skinny joints, berets and coffee shops
keep a bespoke Bebop vibe alive.

Over on Bleeker St, a hint of the Thirties:
plastic bags tumbleweed over
the broad, empty tarmac, as if
a black saloon car is about to appear,
leaking oil and gangsters down the main drag
of some anonymous mid-western town.
Looks like no one's heard of branding here,
just cheap white goods and loud guitars,

but step into CBGB's for a beer
and they're selling Omfug T-shirts at the bar:
six colours, four styles, four sizes.
Because America was built to shop in,
and when Century 21, the world's greatest
discount department store,
re-opens right next to Ground Zero,
the city's wound begins to heal.

Because, hey, it all comes back to the now.
Like rings in a tree trunk that craves your initials,
whirlpooling grooves on an album
scratched by DJ *No Way*,
the streets of New York suck you in
to the fresh, crunchy core of 'Hey, *wow*':
tarted up, chilled out, jazzed over and over —
temptation, oblivion, flowers.

Ground Zero

No more explosions.
The wrecking ball hits a desk
Papers flutter down.

Childless

By slowly growing choice, I have no child
to harbour from the aftershocks of war
waged on, beyond, and in the name of terror,
planting bombs in all the sockets of my home.
If bored with school today, my child could surf the Net
and watch a screaming man being severed from his head.

Instead, I set my latte down, interrupt my head-
long breakfast of the paper, stare at someone else's child.
His name, Nick Berg, a plastic knife, sawing at a net
of lies, glaring as the orange boiler suit he wore.
Today an empty womb becomes my home:
the membrane of a hidden cell that will never split and tear.

For flesh dividing is the beginning of terror
I'm only just able to bear. Embedded in my head
like mines, images of other lives make themselves at home:
an armless boy, a bulldozed girl, a stunted child
who straps explosives to his chest and walks to war,
crying for his mother when the soldiers close the net.

All these amputated stories, caught inside a net,
drag me underneath a sea of ancient errors—
as on its wrinkled surface, the slick spill of this war
slaps and swills against my head.
If I did break down and have a child
would its cradle be a boat to guide me home?

And if I ever did alight upon this land called 'home',
who could calculate the value, gross and net,
of the lives of its inhabitants, down to the last child,
or weigh this worth against the terror
of a stranger's brutal death? Who tots up every head-
line in the daily spreadsheets of this war?

The waitress brings the bill. I stuff the war
into my bag, for the recycle bin at home,
cycle back along the seafront, head
down against the wind. Kids kick balls into a net.
Everything is as it always is; I coast on *terra firma*;
watch TV on the sofa; hug a cushion like a child.

An ever-rising tide, the war engulfs my maisonette:
spineless heads of state spurt the terms of terror
that seeps into my home until there's no room for a child.

Route 24

The woman is sitting upstairs, at the back
of the bus. She has a rucksack.
She is reading the Koran. She is rocking
back and forth. She is shaking.

The man watches, waits. Across the city,
his boss is checking the woman's text messages.
The man's gun aches for his hand.
                    He is sweating.

This is his job. He has no choice.
Since the world began it has been juddering
toward its unmaking.

The anonymous face of an 'appropriate force',
his doubts, if not fears, are long gone.
He scarcely has time for regretting

fatal mistakes that were nobody's fault.
False alarms in his earpiece sound again
and again. But redemption is there
                    for the taking.

The woman is sitting upstairs, at the back
of the bus. She has a rucksack.
She is reading the Koran. She is rocking
back and forth. She is shaking.

[and 13 Israelis]

*In 23 days: over 1300 Palestinians were murdered (over 400 children
and 100 women) and 5300 were injured. Donate your status:
http://apps.facebook.com/supportgaza*

Donate your status.
Donate your despair.
Donate your boyfriend, your girlfriend, your husband, your wife.
Donate your children.
Donate a hospital.
Donate one thousand three hundred and thirteen candles.
Donate a match.
Match a donation.
Donate the fine line between you and your neighbour.
Donate a bucket of soil, a packet of seeds.
Donate a truckload of doughnuts.
Donate a moment of doubt.
Donate your most sophisticated haircut.
Donate a crate of sophistry-detectors.
Donate your will to survive.
Do not do nothing.
Donate your body temperature.
Donate your kidney.
Donate your library.
Donate your deepest desire.
Do not fear ridicule, rage, isolation.
Donate a kilo of rice.
Donate a tenner.
Donate a round table.
Donate the freedom you'd forgotten you had.
Donate your shopping list – your love of avocados, Sharon fruit
and dates.
Donate the sweater your grandmother made you.
Donate a winter of warm, sleepless nights.
Donate a new notion of 'nation'.
Donate a persistent belief that, despite all evidence to the contrary,
everyone, everywhere, is extraordinary.
Donate an hour of your day
to stand up and demonstrate
peace is a process of learning to listen,
and giving is not 'giving in'.

Not A/Haibun
After a talk by Ewa Jasiewicz, Brighton, April 28th 2009

Blonde, porcelain-skinned, wearing denim, a shawl and granny glasses:
she's a young Meryl Streep, fresh from the set of *Mamma Mia* — not
four and a half months in Gaza. The projector isn't working so, her
words precise and technical, her voice striking soft, clear notes that
fill the Friends' Meeting House like the scent of lime blossom, she
speaks for an hour without slides. About

> Mahmoud
> dismembered on his birthday
> in his mother's sweetshop.

A family of seven decapitated in their apartment building stairwell.
The paramedic who trained her, his wife, and half his colleagues,
blown apart in broad daylight beside his ambulance — the Red
Crescent on its roof starkly visible to the F-16 above.
Listening intently, to news of
cancer patients denied treatment; grieving brothers who've joined
the armed resistance; a farmer shot last week for the crime of picking
lentils,

> we taste
> the solitary olive on the tongue
> of the Palestinian prisoners

— the only food the men were given for two days: fruit, not of
mockery, but the trees that had always sheltered them from soldiers,
hunger, the sun. And as the speaker describes how Nizar Rayyan,
his four wives and eleven children refused to leave their home and
became raw hunks of rubble, we remember again the meaning of
al Nakba, and learn that in Gaza in January most people killed were
killed in their homes. While the survivors are still living in tents,
refused concrete and glass for rebuilding, or afraid to return to
the farms near the borders, patrolled by snipers extending their

range into a new No-Go Zone

                    tangentially like the one that
slices through the Meeting House
                when a wiry-haired Northerner
sticks up his hand, denounces Hamas
           as a 'virulent nationalist movement'
   that 'history shows will only
           become as violent as the regime it …'
and in the front row a young Palestinian
           whips round and bellows:

    'THAT'S *ENOUGH.*'

The questioner insists on his right to state his opinion.

One by one people stand
   and politely rebut him
      for being 'overly divisive';
     'judging people who live in unimaginable conditions';
         'not respecting free elections'.

The words
solidarity, oppressor, occupation
hang in the air:
familiar as parents' voices,
the Lord's Prayer.

Shifting her shawl, the speaker argues that Hamas is still making the transition from resistance movement to government, then, raising her voice, urges us to forget boycotts and marches, sacrifice our liberty, smash the weapons makers.

The audience smartly applauds. But privately I wonder why Hamas doesn't just blast through the Wall again and for a moment I wish I was Jewish, had a language in which to ask

                                    Israel, why
                               can't you see
                          the burning anguish,
                           the hatred you sow
             with your white phosphorus and drones?

And looking again at this astonishing young woman, who isn't
dancing all night on a Greek beach, but attaching names to body parts
in a sixty year old war, I hope she too is getting help to cope with *a
post-traumatic shock syndrome to which there is no 'post'.*

The money bucket jangles behind me. The audience shuffles out to
the tea room to argue. But I was brought up a Quaker, and I keep my
silence, bung a fiver toward a portable heart monitor, and come home
to write yet another

                    poem that isn't a poem,
                         asks questions
                    with too many answers,
                       in a wavering voice
               dangerously close to my own.

An Open Poem to Fred Voss —
True Poet and Aerospace Engineer

Dear Fred —
been reading your poems
in all the best magazines,
loving their sinew and sweat,
comradeship, factory floor politics, no bullshit lit crit —
but, hey, it's only just clicked…
fighter jets?
Poet to poet,
womano a mano,
isn't that beyond heavy machinery?
More like an insupportable load?
Buffing those casings, cinching those rivets
pays peanuts, you tell us,
so yeah, that question
you ask more and more often …
why *are* you doing it?
Polishing bomb hatches
with the warm beam of your humanity?
Is it to trouble PhD poets like me?
Force us to see
that we all 'have to murder to live in this world'?
Well, sure …
my own dreams die daily
as I bite that soiled coin,
pay my dirty bills,
use three planets' worth of electricity
to do the dishes every night …
but my bluestockings are laddered and stained
by the bramble bushes surrounding the weapons factory
on Brighton's Home Farm Road,
formerly EDO, of the 'Smash EDO' campaign,
now, since the buy-out, ITT, of the SHUT ITT banners and kites
flopsy-haired kids fly every Wednesday from 4 to 6 pm
while their parents bang pots and pans, blow whistles, chant
   through a megaphone
the names and numbers of the dead
in Gaza, Iraq, Afghanistan,

clanging, whistling, booing and intoning the loudest
when the factory workers finish their shifts,
step out into the car park and hop in their Hondas
behind the spiked green fence
that didn't stop the six Decommissioners
from breaking into that blank-faced building one January night
and smashing EDO for real ... machinery, equipment, computers,
    windows,
trashed to the tune of three hundred grand ...
significantly halting production
of my little city's very own war crimes:
those ERU-151 Bomb Rack Ejector Release Units
and Zero Retention Force Arming Units
that fit so neatly in the F-16 Twin Store Bomb Carriers
that drop a double whammy of death and desolation
on the innocent, far away men, women and children
inconveniently living
on land someone else wants
to control.

Because some of us are still innocent.
Maybe not you or me, or any poet who ever drew breath,
but some of us.
That's why I slammed a rock against a railing today
until it crumbled in my hand,
my butter-soft hand
that's never done a day's hard labour in its life —
though I did like the lathe in high school,
feeling the whirring curve of the bowl emerge
from the pressure I placed on the chisel,
so I get the attraction to mechanical action ...
but Fred, isn't there
no money and endless poetry
in wind turbines, space craft, ambulances, even cranes? —
like the one I climbed with Benjy all those years ago, sitting out on
    the arm
over a snow-dusted Saskatoon street
smoking a joint,
not looking down,
and not knowing

I'd spend my whole life trespassing
in an 8 x 11 inch construction site,
nicking the best workers' tools,
scratching my name on the scaffolding,
and swinging out on a limb, time and again,
to spray paint crazy, heartfelt things like
Fred, I know I've never met you,
never walked a mile in your steel-capped boots,
never even read *Moby Dick*,
but you're a true poet,
so please forgive me when I say
I wish you'd quit your job:
all us gate-bashing noise-niks, hope hammerers, and peace police
need you
on our side
of the fence.

How it happens here

After 'To Shoot An Elephant': a film made in Gaza during Operation Cast Lead.

'The people here can speak for themselves'

but I can't speak to them

the children are playing outside the house

in their language, in their country

The bomb falls

I am not permitted

the mother is running and running, cradling her son

the Home Office says

the father is running and running, clutching his daughter

read the website.

the doctors snatch the children from

the lady in the Lotus Hotel lobby tells me

rush into the hospital

you don't need to go to Gaza

thin white curtains

we don't go to Gaza

strip off the boy's puffy coat

our government says it's not safe

lift him up by the ankles, wrap him up in a sheet

you should call your father, find your family

just his smudged face

go home

for his father to kiss

lady, my family knows who they are

The doctors pinch the little girl's cheek

and they know where I am

shove a tube up her left nostril

in another country again

blood gushes into the tube

where cats are sacred, scrounge garbage

pump her chest, pump her chest

cars are towed screaming, rear wheels locked

stop, rip out the tube

camels are skinned in the market

swaddle her away like her brother

and I wait outside the Embassy in a wicker chair

as the camera hovers and shakes

a dust skeleton gathering on the back of my coat

[47]

How can it be? No blood
on their bodies. No wounds.
Their clothes just a little sooty, that's all.

How can they be tucked away, two to a drawer,
cocooned like papooses, enfolded
in cloud, in the chitons of the gods,

their collapsed faces peeking out,
like the death portraits of mummies,
cheeks swiftly claimed by their skulls?

Now I know.
This is how it happens here.
No coffins. No pall bearers.

Like nannies changing nappies,
old men creasing origami fish,
chefs pinching pastries —

twirling and twisting
plump little dough-moons,
floppy round pitas —

the bombs fling the children into the air,
whip them up in white sheets,
and drop them

into the arms of their parents.
Who clasp the starched parcels
like newborns.

Who must lay their dead
down on the ground
and kneel

for one last,
quick
kiss.

Isma'il Talal Shehda Hamdan, Boy, 9, Civilian
Lama Talal Shehda Hamdan, Girl, 4, Civilian
Haya Talal Shehda Hamdan, Girl, 12, Civilian

I dream Dad's having lunch with Gandhi and ignores me

Fares Tala'at Asa'ad Hammouda, Boy, 2, Civilian
Mohammed Tala'at Asa'ad Hammouda, Boy, 17, Civilian

staggering through Ramses Metro

Sha'aban 'Adel Hamed Hanif, Boy, 16, Civilian
Lina Abdul Menem Hassan, Girl, 10, Civilian
Mohammed Faraj Isma'il Hassouna, Boy, 16, Civilian

a rolled up mattress on my shoulders

Khalil Mohammed Khalil Helles, Boy, 16, Civilian
Mohammed Samir Hijji, Boy, 16, Civilian
Shahad Mohammed Amin Hijji, Girl, 3, Civilian
Hassan Nasim 'Amer Hijo, Boy, 16, Civilian

heavier and heavier, until I fall to my knees

Ahmed Jaber Jabr Howeij, Boy, 6, Civilian

O Lady of the Lotus Hotel Lobby

Isma'il 'Adnan Hassan Hweila, Boy, 16, Civilian

I don't know if I'm going up or down

Hamam Issa, Boy, 1, Civilian

I won't know till I'm there

Abdul Rahman Ibrahim Tawfiq Jaballah, Boy, 14, Civilian
Mahmoud Mohammed Mahmoud Jaballah, Boy, 14, Civilian
Fatima Raed Jadullah, Girl, 10, Civilian
Ahmed Rasmi Mohammed Abu Jazar Boy, 16, Civilian
Abdullah Jihad Hussein Juda, Boy, 15, Civilian
Mahmoud Ahmed Fares Juha, Boy, 16, Militant

We Are Coming To Gaza

After The Gaza Freedom March in Cairo, Dec 2009.
organised by the American activist group Code Pink.

We are coming to Gaza
from different places.

Some of us were born in the tunnels
that feed Palestine with Northern Irish blood;
others have further to travel.

Some are crossing an ocean of assumptions.
Some picking their way through a minefield
of qualms and shifting ideals. A few are blogging
en route, juggling PR jargon and CNN headlines.

Many are breasting the Third Wave
of another global struggle —
until our sisterhood crashes on a thirty-foot wall
and trickles down into a no-man's land
of summary executions and scrap metal.

Forsaking the thin air of neutrality,
cresting the moguls of four languages,
a team of young idealists
slaloms down the mountains of Geneva.

Others are striding through the clear air of the Highlands;
rising up from the pavement silhouettes of Hiroshima;
or sailing round the Cape of Good Hope
in *The Amandla Intifada*;

Above us, a man is airlifting his wounded buddies
from the rice paddies of Nam.
In front of us, an eighty-five year old woman
is carrying the hunger of Auschwitz
in her belly — it roars as she walks,
like an awakening lion.

And when we are stopped in a blaring Cariene square,

kettled by squads of baby-faced riot police,
some of us dance, hand-in-hand,
to the husky music of a Rabbi's voice,
the gusty lungfuls of a stomach Steinway from Vermont,
the gift of a German fiddle
donated by the toe-tapping folk of East Sussex.

While, yes, the French are insatiable —
fuelled on pizza, truffles and five o'clock prayers,
they chant, rap and drum all night, every night,
to keep the pavement warm
for those returning to a homeland
they've never been allowed in,
waiting to sear with the tears of arrival
the cheeks of families and friends
they've never met.

And as our movement dawns
and the barricades tighten,
then open a crack, to admit just
'the sincere humanitarians'
and bar all 'hooligans and trouble-makers' …
                someone from an empire
                with a thousand borders but no bounds,
                barges to the head of the queue —
while others from his shores, at last,
blush the colour of their bright pink T-shirts
turn and listen to those
who have never stopped saying:

We are coming to Gaza together.
We are coming for the Gazans.

Because we did not come for the Armenians.
Because we came too late for the Jews.

And if we do not come now, together,
Gaza will soon be a cemetery
a livid scar in our memories,
a strip of flesh ripped
from the numb conscience of the world.

Rhetorical Devices

And if the Palestinians had entered Jerusalem
every third Saturday, alone or in families,
walked calmly to markets or synagogues,

then blown a shrill whistle, gripped detonators,
and letting shoppers and worshippers scatter,
graffiti'd the air with only their own blood?

> *Gaza, Gaza, do not cry*
> *We will never let you die*

> *From the river to the sea*
> *Palestine, you will be free*

Would Israel still have built the wall?
Or paved 'Martyrs' Square' in gold and sold tickets?
And we? Would we still have stormed City Hall,
firing our peaceable rockets?

God Save Our Noble Team

It's not just the wiggling hips of the Nigerians,
the young dog stamina of the South Koreans,
the street urchin haircuts of the Irish,
the sultry glowers of the Azzurri's finest,
or the pristine thighs and jaws
they all possess by right.
Nor is it all down to Beckham's honeyed torso,
Quinny's height and lilt,
Rivaldo's shark-like teeth,
Rio's languid flair,
Ronaldhino's girlie locks —
or even Fabien's bum being spritzed with cold spray
during a constipated bout with Italy back in '98.
It's almost but not quite the Argentines' black socks,
long locks and grizzled chins,
and it just, just barely isn't the passing fancy
of being hired to alleviate Harry Kewell's groin strain
with Tantric warm-up exercises
that traps me in front of the telly
each time a World Cup football match is played.

Yes, footballers are sexy.
Some are compact and keep their shape
—except in the second half—
some have 'individual skills' to die for,
others keep clean linen sheets.
And even though their shorts were shorter
back in Guadalajara,
their kit is really cute and shows off their physiques.
And yes, they run around in the heat and wet,
stripping off their shirts
every time they score.

But truly, it's the game they play that turns me on.

It's the time football takes,

the beautiful, agonising length of it —
two or three hours prone on my futon,
waiting, wanting, yearning for one elusive goal,
never knowing how or when
the next stroke of panic, misery or euphoria will fall:
all attention focused
on the flickering of the screen, the flicking of the ball.
It's the lull of knowing there is nothing more
and nothing less important than the voyage of that ball,
hurtling like pleasure, like pain,
from player to player,
down the electric green grass
in search of the back of the net
one goal
being sometimes technically sufficient,
but never quite enough.

Yes, football is sex.
And with its side netting, woodwork and offside traps,
it can get pretty kinky.
But it is also love, history, religion, commerce, politics, art, war,
    dance,
and a way — for now— to keep the Americans in the dark.
A sport so simple little plastic men can play it,
so epic that every four years it hurls nations into riots
of bloodlust, revenge, inspiration, celebration and bitter cursing of
    the gods.
Football gathers up like sweaty rags
the orgiastic revelry of the fans,
the irrevocable decisions of the referees,
the irreversible moments of good or bad luck —
and on the solipsistic reverie of the screen
wrings out a passionate meditation upon fate.
Football is a bad marriage in a Catholic country.
Football is the sanctity of human error.
Football is the tedium of the commentators' inane obsessions
crowding out one's own.
Football is a game played on dirt in the townships,
the temporary triumph of immigrant labourers

and the brutal crush of the media machine.
Football is a gladiators' ring of fancy boys and immortals.
Football is NAFTA with cleats.
Football is a rum-soaked trifle,
a Christmas tin of Quality Street chocolates,
lobster and champagne.
Football is Seaman's tear-stained sheet.
Football is Escobar's own goal.
Football is the letter you shouldn't have opened.
Football is the speed at which you realise
your entire life has been undone.

The Turning Point

Before she shags the lads
And gets slagged out of Margate.
See the Swedish policeman savage the jockey
Before he carries him from the van

And lays him gently in the road.
Watch the spindly tree spinning like a top
Before the moody man looks out the window
In Gallery Movie Land.

You always enter the room
In the middle of the film, sit down on the floor,
Watch until the end. Then hang about
To catch up on what you missed

See half of LA Raeven slouch on the sill
Before she slouches on the chair.
Watch famous Tracey dancing, joyful in reprisal,
Before she shags the lads

Teutonic Shifts

Ten years ago, Autonomen & angels ruled Berlin.
Grandmothers in bondage frocks skateboarded to lesbian balls;

acrid felines strafed the night city skies; and one sunny morning
people built and ate a wall of jammy bread. In London,

Neubauten jack-hammered the ICA, drilling through the floor
to the subterranean corridor that connects Buck Palace and the Mall.

The gallery pulled the plug at damage of three grand.
The band, booked as a 'theatre of destruction', burned the bill.

Today the work is monochromatic, non-catastrophic.
Trippy Techno. V1-rockets resembling little wooden fish.

A Stasi recreation camp in evening light:
pink and yellow as a slice of Battenberg cake.

In the front seat of a Mini Cooper, I watch a windscreen video
—Heidegger dubbed over beach blanket bingo—

and wish I was back in a Trebbie, the cardboard car I drove
around the Last Watchtower, a concrete turret squatted

by a gang of Ossi art punks, who hung photos of their mates
hurling pfennigs out of windows to a desperate, scrabbling crowd.

But now Berlin is squeaky clean, phenomenology is fun,
palace skivvies running errands fear not Krautrock attack:

wanting cabaret and urban angst is like craving acid at a rave.
Get with it, girl. Crunch that Ex-Stasi.   At last,

the crate. Thin, peeling slats. An egg storage building unmade
into a fragile incubator for infertile souls. I can live with that.

Ancient History

Assyrian warriors planned invasions twice: once sober,
once drunk. Swimming the Tigris hugging goats' bladders
they prayed for giant angels to guide them after death
through iron gates now standing in a museum corridor.

Desert wolves, they ruled their age, with savage pride creating
Babylon and cuneiform tableaux — the virtues of their king
crosshatched across his portrait, as if an army of small birds
had marched a hymn of praise upon his stage.

The Assyrians were also early body sculpture artisans,
from cypress sap and camel tongues engineered machines
to build their calves into the shape of conch shells,
the trumpets of their Gods ...or so I whisper in your ear...

as in this hall of infidels, I pause, trying not to hold you —
who once harnessed every natural force to come down on my fold.

Musée de Moyan Âge

We came here years ago, during our summer of lusting
in Montmartre; we sheltered from the sun in rooms
of broken statues, tapestries and toothless ivory combs.
Now I drip down all the halls, in another scorching August,

searching for the Lady in her gardens of red grass.
The unicorn, I can report, is still as horny as a goat:
her fingers smooth his mane, his hooves disturb her skirt.
I know her shadowed eyes from my own looking glass,

but cannot cool my molten body in her blue retreat
nor enter the pavilion that flows around her like the sea,
'*A Mon Seul Desir*' stitched in gold across its folds.

You are back in London, sprinkling roses in the heat.
I'm burning up, a cinder from a blazing masterpiece —
or just a smudge upon a postcard, your mistress growing old.

English Eccentrics in Love

Not just his tiger rugs and scorpions,
all of Stanley Spencer's paintings make me think of you:
their rich palette like the quarried colours
of your kisses; their untamed quaintness
like the way you sometimes brush your hair.

Somehow I imagine he'd approve of your desire
to start a new religion, just to worship women. When the virgin
Stanley married Hilda, he painted the Resurrection
in his village churchyard: souls arising from the soil
in tribute to the earthly succour of his wife.

After the divorce, though, he fell
hard for a dyke, painted Patricia naked
beside a leg of mutton, his own ineffectual
appendages—glasses, genitals, head—dangling
blue and strangled over her supine disdain.

I'm sure you would have warned him, but
when Stan offered his model all his money and his house
Patricia and her lover had a little chat, agreed
she would accept his ring of heartfelt truth,
and walk the aisle with him.

Stanley slept with Hilda on the wedding night.
Pat scarpered six months later (back to Dorothy's warm bed),
unperturbed by carnal knowledge of our man,
who wrote love letters to his Hilda
for years beyond her death.

Who'd choose to be a painter or a muse? God knows
I smiled when you announced your chosen deity. But
though gold rings have never come between us at the altar
we anoint; though women are to me as well the staff of life;
still I suffer like a wife the fluctuations of your faith.

Leaves tremble, water shimmers when we touch,
swans sail down our river in the night.
But the red brick walls of factories and chimney stacks
bulge between us in the moonlight
when you rise to go back home before the dawn.

Perhaps I do deserve someone unswerving, who'll build me up
with patient brushstrokes in his heart. But if you did
would I adopt Patricia's joyless gaze:
irritated icon, shark in lace garters,
martyr to the marriage bed, a girls' girl to the end?

Late Works
for Catherine Lupton

I

September 13th 2001. Catherine's father, having seen
his garden finished, laboured for his breath.
Beneath station concourse screens, America in flames,
she pelted for three trains: arrived scant hours late

Did catastrophe overtake him?
                          Or was that lost goodbye
tempered by a deep paternal instinct, to shield her
with his body, from the media fusillade?

Perhaps, like my mother, dying as comets plunged into Jupiter,
he yoked his immolation to a historical collision
in order to console. Stars, planets, nations, women, men,
must all someday be engulfed. No mourner is alone.

II

A fortnight after incomprehensible events
Catherine and I set out for Kent.
In a Folkestone gallery on the Leas
Derek Jarman and his fate were wrestling in paint.

The day was a grey curtain, on the wrong side
of the windows. We wandered
toxic symphonies of colour, dissonant overload.

IMPOTENT   PUS   TRAGEDY

    BUBBLE AND SQUEAK   DOOLALLY

proclaimed the massive canvases,
the black words savaged
by galactic spasms, projectile spews,
lurid contortions, bedpans full of psychotropic worms
thick enough to eat, a crimson carpet-bombing
of Daily Mail campaigns to 'name and shame'.

    LOVE   SEX   DEATH

Hurt eyes. Angry leavings.
                  SPREAD THE PLAGUE
And then:

             OH ZONE

the light
lambent on the water (the view from Dungeness?)

III

Scoured by raucous beauty, faces shining in the cold,
we crossed the promenade, made our way down to the shore.

The sea was falling, fiery white, an open-hearted moan —
I followed Catherine as she walked into the thin arms of the rain.

Sefton Park
for Sarah Hymas

We take a bus from Paradise Station
down a road Sarah dreamed of two nights ago
— Caesar's Palace on the corner, art deco
wrought iron next door — a street she'd never been on
before we came to Liverpool.

The bus sails down through sunny Toxteth,
where I lived for a month in the Seventies,
a social worker's child, at home in a halfway house.
I remember a wedding just after we arrived:
a bountiful black woman, her chipper Irish groom,
faces beaming with the most happiness I'd ever seen —
a joy that made me hide behind my Mum,
as if the bride was going to float away like a balloon.

Sarah knows Toxteth because of the Eighties'
riots, ten years after I left,
a melancholy bed wetter, already a veteran
of two continents in seven years, now en route to a third:
not a Scouser exactly, after only three years Merseyside,
but an ardent Kevin Keegan fan,
John Lennon waiting to claim me in my teens.

Is it memories or cine footage
that leap up at the bus windows like playful dogs
when we pass the mock-Tudor library?
Its black timbers and white walls,
unlikely fairytale sweetness,
announcing the nearness of Sefton Park:
place where all is forgiven,
and all forget how to despair,
place of blowing bubbles in the nude.

On the map the park's an embryo,
nurtured by an artery of residential road.

We enter down at Aigburth Vale, walk up
along the boating lake, laughing at the ducks.
The crocuses are out: yolk-yellow,
royal purple, egging on the daffs.
In the city spring comes early
Sarah says, thanks to car exhaust.

But Sefton Park accepts no contradictions.
In Sefton Park, everyone and everything is whole
and perfect, just as creation intended us to be.
In Sefton Park, I could believe in God.

We have a purpose; we are moving to the Dell,
visiting the Palm House on the way —
newly reopened, all fresh paint and shining glass,
sultry climes and rich green hanging plants,
it's a transparent, botanic version of Paddy's Wigwam:
Liverpool's twin temples of glory in the round.

Outside again, hot cheeks freshened by the air,
we venture down an avenue of Scotch fir,
to the very heart of Sefton Park:
a shady grove, a stream, a lover's bridge,
a wooded hollow from whence life's water springs.
It's too early for the tumbling blossoms I remember,
someone's left his trainer in the grotto,
there's a smell of damp and mould, but the Dell
is always fertile, always magic — today
we are anointed like two snowdrops in its knoll.

All that's left now is a stroll across the meadow,
the level playing fields where once I ran and squealed,
only embarrassed of my nakedness when policemen came in view.

It's boggy in the grass, so we walk along the paths
up to Croxteth Drive, at the bus stop ask advice
on how to find the Tate.

It's the fifth time we've stopped a passer-by today.

Because isn't it wonderful to be back in Liverpool
where everyone talks like the Beatles:
• flocks of mockneys chattering and chirping
in Lime Street and Lark Lane,
giving long, sometimes wholly wrong directions
to places they are part of, but have only been to in a dream.

Shape Maven
after Barbara Hepworth

Some said her work was cold, untouchable.
But now for her centenary, the Tate St Ives
studs the galleries with guards
to keep our hands away from her
glossy contours, chiselled ripples
silent strings. We are greasy. We exude
ice-cream, lotions, rain. We mustn't
touch even her holes today.

In the 'Scented Guarea' room
I lean forward, sniffing. The guard laughs.
Two more inches and I could have kissed the wood.
As the feet of sinners arch to meet
the dry lips of a saint, I seek the impersonal
benediction at her core —
the heart of the pure whole note
she held in the throat of the world.

The Coastal Path

Ahead of me, the cormorants
bow their black necks,
two slick stitches disappearing
into the wrinkles of the sea.
Humid with waiting, my eyes dip
heavy-lidded into mist,
emerge with bellies full of ink
and moistened paper fish.

Stoats dart over, under and around
the shoreline's weighted hem of rocks,
pert tails whisking away the loose
thread-ends of crevice, nostril, paw.
When we are the only mammals left
I flash for a self-timer camera,
turn my spine of sea-shells to the lens.
The frisky couple stare and snap at flies.

Lightly redressed, on the crest of the land,
I sing a lament for my mother.
The kestrel hangs —
a raised eyebrow,
missed heartbeat
— by a strand of grey hair
in the air.

This time an empty beak, a new wind.
If I were a small frightened animal
I would vanish quickly too:
beaded with bright yellow snails,
ruffled with field mice, sweating slugs,
the path is a butcher's bridal train.
I carry no brush to sweep it free of life.
Every tenth boot step is a sickening crunch.

The slow and helpless are sacrificed for my horizon.

A giantess returning to her headland,
ignoring the garish tents and windbreaks
pulped beneath her tread, I leave
an oozy trail of splintered shelter in the grass,
scrape my heart clean on the view.
I do not stop. I have no child.
I stride, embroidering the distance to my death.

Swimming at Land's End

I did it to deserve a brandy,
to sleep more soundly,
to wear my new bikini,
to make the most of my holiday,
to spit in the eyes of the rain.

I did it to strip off my sweater,
clammy T-shirt, muddy jeans,
to reveal white limbs, scarlet two-piece:
a goose-pimpled lighthouse
unblinking on the beach.

Bare skin defying wet-suited bluster,
chasing a fast retreating tide,
I did it to run down sloping sand,
to feel the packed wet beach
absorb the depression of my feet.

Shivering, I did it, to trigger an icy shock,
to feel cold escalate in conscious waves
from knees to ribs to neck,
exposing underwater cells
to the tingling miracle of heat.

Finally, I did it: to spur the rictus grin
of triumph over inertia, over surfers,
to split my face wide open
like a dark cloud
suddenly emblazoned by the sun.

The Jellyfish

A giant's eye unmoored, blind, avoiding dreams.
A glob of purple Semtex, exploded in a sealed up, soundproof
    room.
A belladonna pudding, flung into the sea.
A cold flophouse.
A bottle cap of phlegm.
The ocean's toxic comet, dragging its lopped tail
    along the coast.
A mermaid's umbrella.
A sea horse's parachute.
An unborn child.
A soft-boiled brain.
A slimy minefield, dumped onto the beach.

The jellyfish spins its own transparency
into the clear, chill waters that surround us.
Human waste drives it far from shore
a balloon escaping our celebrations
to drift with seaweed, fish and foam.

I mustn't touch it
or it will forget how to swim.
No wonder its frills contract like petticoats
as it torpedoes away from danger.
But caught in the swell of a wave
the jellyfish dances the slowest of tarantellas
swaying with the ghosts of its lovers and children
like the great, drooling tears of the moon

The Nude Beach

It is night. I am miles from the beach.
Concrete miles and cold months. It is winter.
But the beach reaches into my bed. The nude beach,
where the sea glistens, retreats, like a teasing silk sheet;
where the sun's a burning lens, filming flint, sand and skin —
and the sky erases everything. The nude beach,
where the men are nude, and the women are nude,
where I am nude and the wind
flickers through me. Where I am a candle flame, and
your shaved balls, tucked between your legs
as you stretch beside your girlfriend,
are blinding orbs of light. Yes, the nude beach
has its chemistry and physics, its history and themes.
The nude beach has 'baked beans' — queens —
al fresco blow jobs, massage hubs, an albino Burmese python.
Here, young Mike leans over to borrow my sun cream,
Hollywood Bob admires my coppery bush,
and you, finally, flinch over the pebbles to show me
your leather cock ring one day, the next
your wounded finger, the tip split open
like a clown's smile where she bit it: a bite
the nurse said was worse than a dog's.
Oh, the nude beach has its dramas and desires,
its bits of rusty metal, glinting glass.
But though the sea pinched my clitoris
and the moon kissed the nape of your neck,
nothing ever truly happens here. For the nude beach only exists
in rippled reflections, off-season evenings — when I am
on the nude beach in my green straw hat and red sunglasses,
six warm plums nestling on my towel, even as your balls
dazzle and blink, both guiding and warning me,
the waves are undressing the shore,
exposing its wet emerald groyne, the dark
clumps of seaweed straggling over the pebbles,
caught in the teeth of the sea:

and it's clear that anything real here
has always already occurred many times over, is lost
in a worn cloud of midges, the faint stink of dulse,
the wavering heat that blankets us all,
makes our nudity a veiled mirage,
the beach my bed of nails.

Unlucky Stars

It was a day when everyone felt unimportant,
vulnerable as kittens in a bag.

Everyone was needy and drawn and close to tears.
Everyone wanted to quit.

Everyone wondered what everyone else really
thought of them. Everyone hated their homes.

Everyone wanted a pet, but the terms of their leases forbade animals.
Anyway, there was no room for a litter box in the loo.

Everyone was working too hard, spending too much.
They just couldn't stop it. As if they'd lived all their lives

without the barest necessities, owed it to themselves to catch up.
No one had taken proper holidays in years.

Everyone was experiencing the putrid sensation of purpose
sliding off their bones like rotten flesh.

Everyone was especially dismal in the mornings.
Coffee only made the sense of irritation worse.

Everyone with children wanted their offspring to shut up, shrink,
crawl back into the womb, devolve into their component
                                        chromosomes.

Everyone else despaired
of ever having a family of their own.

Everyone was tired of being ignored, or taken for granted;
but had no real hope of getting lasting recognition.

Everyone with money felt tight and resentful of everyone without
                                        money.
Everyone without money felt fragile and despised.

Everyone was highly intelligent and resourceful.
Nobody knew what to do.

There weren't enough gardens, or nice days in the year.
There weren't any cures for Aids, herpes, depression, or war.

There weren't any profit margins in cures.
Everyone was sick at heart for the benefit of the economy.

Everyone fruitlessly compared themselves to their friends.
Everyone had forgotten the taste of joy.

Just an ordinary day.
Without mercy, miracles, or end.

Sitting in the Window of Al Casbah Restaurant

Waiting for someone who never calls,
I check my mobile, touch up my lipstick,
twist a paper napkin into a swan.
Outside, in the faintly glazed day,
Hampstead High Street is a concrete catwalk
of fur hats, Ugg boots, tassled leather bags,
diamante muzzles, flowered wellies, baby buggies:
incognito celebs and designer shop assistants
pouting toward Starbucks to be bored.
I take a sip of mint tea.
An old woman in a faded Mac
appears on the other side of the glass.
Her face a crumpled moon, she's leaning
on a younger, ginger version of herself.
Blotchy-cheeked, her eyes round as pennies,
the daughter nestles closer
as, with arthritic grace, her mother
points out the *shisha* between us,
tracing the curves of its serpentine nozzle,
silver bowl for fruit tobacco,
bulbous water chamber.
I know that I am gaping.
I want the world to stop.
These two small, homely people
are radiant, lit from within by gladness
to be alive, to be together. They laugh
and it's clear, the street's smoky blend
of SUV fumes, stale Chanel and January damp
is the freshest air they've ever breathed.
Wrapped up warmly in each other,
they leave me stranded in my seat,
the daughter rolling on the edges of her feet,
her hands cramped underneath her wrists
like the beaks of beautiful birds.

The London Fleadh
i.m Kirsty MacColl

It rained and wouldn't stop, for Neil Young or for God.
The mud, the mud was thick as fudge around the stage
it made my feet a pair of bogs, and stole the whole damn show.

Siobhan and I beneath a tree, squabbling over lipstick,
watched a lad heave-ho his lass above the marsh,
then drop her three steps later into ploppy disbelief.

The girls fought back in packs, pelting every man in sight,
then, baring pointed teeth and chocolate-coated palms,
streaked Cadbury's fingers down our cheeks.

Dancing above us, an exaltation of silver balloons,
Kirsty's voice pierced the clouds, commanded the sun:
the squelchy field lit up like a polished bar room floor.

Shaking our rain-sequined brollies, we sang *Sonny Jim*.
Siobhan in the cowboy hat she'd blagged off the Greeks
me in a bin bag, and cowpats for boots.

Together we waltzed in a quagmire, tangoed and dipped,
slipping and catching each other in time—Siobhan's hot
orange smile triggering my smeared crimson grin.

The Find
for Mat

The day they cracked the squat
like an egg
like a whip

you slung your sleeping bag and rucksack
in a small back room
and headed for the attic

treading with your torch across the beams
searching for the bounty
tucked beneath the eves

opening the suitcase meant for you to find
with its barely audible cargo
of tape reels

and the obsolete machine that spun them into sound.
The building's time capsule
of static and old voices

the emptiness it harboured, splintered
like a broken-into shell
a cat o' nine tails rumour

of a place people forgot to live in, opening its doors
rewinding all the half-erased
space beneath its roof.

Secretary to the Sea

Shop windows tide her over
lonely evenings on the town:
from rows of silver seashells
she picks out her next phone.

Sighing in her bedroom
— will she ever earn enough? —
she folds her clothes like unread notes
of resignation; love.

In the morning at the bus stop
she aches to stay awake;
hot coffee at the office
jolts her head above the waves.

For if the sirens claimed her,
if she stopped treading water,
the fish would drown, the moon turn brown
the ocean's heartbeat falter.

The Arsonist

Some said
it was the starling-shit
combusting: like a Buddhist nun
the old pier set herself alight.
By noon, a whitewash sky
has lowered on her protest —
just another cloudy day,
with a wrongly
autumn scent.

Later, though,
a blue-black evening
frames her
smouldering pall.
Floorboards snap
like castanets,
and from her blistered sides
firefalls of sparks
rain like kamikaze woodlice
down into the sea.
Above the waves
her iron bones
stand in an ovation
to the night.

On the beach
I sit and watch
the darkness flow
into the shadow of a man
diving from her ribcage:
a charcoal after-image
of my own thirst
to burn.

The Pablo Neruda Barbeque

Poets, singers, newly weds,
gather on the beach,

share olives, wine, guitars,
books and bits of Spanish,

poke sausages with skewers,
orchestrate umbrellas.

Softly rumbling clouds,
charcoal, seared with gold,

fill their bellies with our smoke.
And when the sky splits open

a tender ray of sunshine
warms our faces as we read

poems of love and tomatoes,
elemental odes —

the white lips of the sea
sucking at the stones.

Brighton Beach

One lone Mod pigeon
struts across the pebbles
black feathers crested with white trim
red legs stepping out.
And just as no true Mod
would ever get sweaty in the dirt
it keeps its distance from the gulls
those raucous rockers
who hold the town to ransom
whenever the rubbish trucks drive by.

There's a parka on the beach today
and my boyfriend's in it
sitting in the rain
with his sleepy, hippie Goth girl
turning up the tape player's
scratchy Northern Soul.

His is a simple philosophy: love
plus the big band theory
of the universe
equals the individual sound
of each and every wave.

The Undertow

Leaning against a parapet
above the evening sea,

we kiss, and watch the waves
race along the groyne:

white slippers
pattering up the cobbles,

frothy dresses
twirling in the air,

again and again, like lovers,
they chase each other to the shore;

until one, all glass
and pebble-dashed,

smacks
back into the onrush —

breaks a dancer's spine
against the wall.

Reaching for your hand,
my lips a salty whirl,

I feel the tide
begin to turn:

dragging at the stones
beneath our feet,

grabbing fistfuls
of the coastline

as we fall.

Peter Crouch
A Tall Story

We would have suffered
tabloid hell,
but if you and I had met
when I first began to bleed,
we could have been his parents,
this gangly, buck-toothed sapling,
long-stemmed flower
of English youth,
six foot six of bashful hope.
He doesn't look like you or me,
or anyone on earth,
but still we call out *gorgeous,*
lovely, well done, son,
as we cuddle on the sofa,
watching Crouchie
chesting and back-heeling it
for Liverpool and country,
stooping, not to conquer
but to assist
the goals of others,
having played 1000 minutes
without one of his own.
He's too nice, the pundits say,
this striker who can't score,
but if he's happy just to play,
it's all our fault, we taught him
everything we know:
how to find your team mates,
trap and flick the ball,
do what brings you joy,
ignore the jingles and the catcalls
in the stands.
And we marvel
every time we see him
that his eager features

are not haunted,
his loping legs not snared
by our dragging, secret fear
of leaving nothing
glorious behind:
thanks to him we feel
that death's a petty thing.
Yes, he's our darling love child:
we fought the law to keep him,
fed him eels and spaghettini,
gave him totem poles
for Christmas,
and now he's shooting
like our hearts,
up above the crossbar
to the stars.

Skin-dipped

Midnight on the heath,
the air as mild as breath,

clothes became superfluous,
we shed them on the grass.

The water, black and supple,
how cold we couldn't tell,

until you jumped into the pond
and jumped right out again.

I swam a steady circle,
disturbing two small birds,

my fingers broken icicles,
my nipples shining nails.

In Finland there's a saying,
throwing off your winter fur;

half-afraid of dying,
as if this were my final year,

I felt the seasons flowing,
my body burning like a star.

Plaka

A fusty tang by the taverna:
feral cats, spying on the diners.
I fed a skinny tabby morsels of moussaka;
she licked clean the oily aubergine,
devoured the meat with pinprick teeth,
then curled up in a chair, spitting
when I tried to stroke her cheek.

Outside, haloed in a streetlight,
swaying to a music all his own,
a blind old man sold coconut crescents
from a basin of miniature fountains:
In sparkling threads of water, a Cartier display,
he washed a chipped white plate,
his brown hands thick with foam.

After coffee we climbed the Acropolis,
squatted under the stars as kids in black jackets
strummed songs we didn't know.
At last, a lemony musk tingeing
the night air, we found a lonely bench,
sat and whispered strange new words
for 'kitten' and 'hello'.

The Holiday

The fifth night in the villa,
sleep is a blanket
kicked to the floor,
love a damp, tangled sheet
I peel from my skin,
leave wrapped around you
in the shuttered room
as I shower your sweat
from my breasts,
stare out the window
at split walnut husks,
pink-crested hills,
the bitter sage of olive trees
tarnishing the dawn.

I flick the switch
and a whirring begins
in the curtains, a warning,
some creature, small and urgent,
hurtling into orbit
round the naked bulb.
Not a moth, a tawny blur,
clinging to a bent black needle,
stabbing at the air —
seeking nectar and direction
from a droplet of the sun,
the hummingbird
thuds against the ceiling,
unable to look down.

*You Never Say Goodbye to a Myth**

Our flight home from Athens
was delayed seven hours,
so we spent our last Euros
on bread rolls and water,
then brandished the plastic
on a Duty Free spree,
and gate-crashed McCafe,
demanding glasses and ice.
Giggling and glowing,
we sat on the orange banquette,
sipping smuggled champagne
and cracking pistachios,
while a Japanese couple
played whist. Pissed with finesse,
discussing how love changes sex,
we kissed until we knew
a creaking bed in a cheap hotel
was not to be the last
Greek temple dedicated to
our metamorphosis.

[*Greek tourist board slogan]

The Minotaur
after the sculpture by Beth Carter

Bronze, doll-sized, down on bended knee,
he holds the frail white hand
of a blindfolded bunny-girl.

'That's you and me,' I tease,
thinking of your bullish need
to point your horn and charge;

those tangled fits of paranoia
that wind me up and dump us
in a cramped and sunless pit;

but also, of your tender courtesies:
warm guitar and patient harmonies
when I sing your songs off-key;

cups of tea and scented pillows
when I wake up screaming
from dreams that you've dismembered me.

You close your eyes and smile.
We both prefer the dark
illusion we are one

to the eruptions of those snorting beasts
bound up in the mazy world
that gleams between the sheets.

In the Lap of the Gods

Look, Zeus.
Laps are for lovers
and children and cats,
not wasted ex-flings,
and blonde bombshell
daughters of dead friends.
Yes, I know you are a lightning rod
for damaged women,
it makes me sad to see them too,
a rash of lost girls, erupting
on the thick skin of the world.
But, trust me,
they've got to find their own boyfriends
to straddle and fondle,
to dandle and cuddle them,
kiss the cuts and bruises on their souls.
It's a hard journey, I know,
I've crawled it backwards, naked,
many times myself,
but you have to nudge them
off your knee
and down that lonely road:
even at birthdays and funerals
your lap is our cradle alone.
For in your lap, wrapped
in the silk purse I gave you,
your genitals lie purring,
dreaming of my hips:
and unless you want to see
the earth rise up in bleeding strips
to burn and flay the sky
into a welter of black dust,
let no other
needy female
disturb
that sacred
sleep.

Merry Crisis

After you arrived
at the airport
three hours early,
and, shuffling inch by inch,
held a place for me
in the queue
rustling through Departures
like a giant length of tinsel;
after that elderly couple
repeatedly jammed
their baggage trolley
into the backs of your legs
then, when you retorted,
tailed you for an hour,
muttering 'foreigner'
while I sulked
because you'd forgotten
my grey skirt; after
removing your watch,
belt and boots, and
telling me you were going
to run through security
peemol naked; after
buying Snow Queen vodka
for Willem, a whiskey cake
for your Mum; after
waiting two hours
in a café overlooking
dark, foggy runways,
checking the monitors
every ten minutes
for a flight first delayed,
delayed again,
then cancelled;
after phoning your mum,
— who cried —
after picking up our luggage
without having gone

anywhere, after waiting
another half hour
in yet another queue,
as two zooming boys
made war, and a family
discovered they had
the wrong red suitcase;
after kissing, whispering
life could be worse;
after meeting
the human face of Easyjet,
a beaming young man
tactfully not in a Santa hat;
after being told
there were no more seats
on any flight tonight
or tomorrow, and anyway,
the staff were going home;
after hauling fragile gifts,
your guitar, a ton of winter
clothes and books
down an unscheduled flight
of stairs and onto a train to
Brighton; after I thwacked
my hot pink suitcase
against a man's foot,
a scruffy bloke
in a fur-trimmed vest,
who laughed when I said
'pink's not for sissies',
causing you to glare
at anyone having fun;
after all that, and more,
eight hours
of transport hell,
when the train
picked up speed
and the bloke and his mate
pulled out tobacco pouches,
you finally exploded:
towered over them in

your ancient sheepskin coat,
bellowed that your
girlfriend was asthmatic
and threatened to stop
the train, which was
already stopping
at Three Bridges,
as the men stubbed
their butts,
raised their hands
in the air, and
the other passengers
fled down the carriage;
and when, yelling
'I've had it!
I've had enough!'
you stuck your head
out the doors
to find a station guard,
and I thought
you might storm off,
so called out *'Paul!'*
and you returned,
glowering to your seat,
I knew exactly how you felt:
though, strangely,
having decided
from the moment
our flight was cancelled
to simply be glad
we hadn't been at Heathrow
— herded into cold marquees
then told that every flight
until the New Year
had been cancelled
and our checked-in luggage
lost —
I myself felt calm
and nurturing,
so even though
I'm not asthmatic,

and I hate it
when you exaggerate,
I hugged you,
curled up in your arms;
and when I opened my eyes,
the bloke we'd both abused
was sitting opposite,
grinning; and with
a gap-toothed gleam,
and boozy breath
told first me, then us,
about his cash job
plumbing in Sandy
— full of 'rum folk' —
and the Christmas dinner
he was planning
for his missus:
a salmon barbie
on the beach,
with mange tout
and baby corn,
something different,
to celebrate their escape
from the skeletons
in the deep-freeze
of their lives
before they met;
and as he talked,
you relaxed,
and even though
I knew it would be me
who'd brave the airline
phone queues
in the morning, make sure
we got to Holland
for your Mum,
I could tell already
we were going to have
a beautiful Christmas—
the omens
were all good.

What's Jung Got To Do With It?

Breaking bread and dipping it in soup,
You say I'm 'very masculine' sometimes.
Argh. I want to gag you with my spoon.

Why does it sound as if you're trying to impugn
Me, accuse me of a raft of gender crimes —
Don't you like it when I dunk you in my soup?

Oh darling, can't you see my lipstick droop,
Detect the lurking lack of chimes,
When you clang that rusty knife against my spoon?

For I feel about as glamorous as a prune
When you prick me with those antique paradigms —
A prune in hobnail boots, drowning in your soup.

If you mean I can be bossy, have been known to swoop
Down on your sins — poppet, think of pantomimes:
A slapstick villainess who spanks you with a spoon;

Peter Pan in tights, singing slightly out of tune.
Men are sharp as lemons; women sting like limes:
So let's bake bread together, make a hearty soup,
Then with cayenne kisses, set fire to my spoon.

In The Square

You dug in a pocket and gave me a crumb.
The man beside me laughed.

You reached in your jacket and pulled out a stone.
The woman behind me coughed.

He's an only child, I cried.
A stout old lady huffed.

Then you thrust your hand in the winter air,
a cold, unfolding fist —

I tossed the crumb to a marble dove,
and kissed your clumsy gift.

Purge-aholics

Why do we always return
to the room where I sob and you snarl?
Is there something we desperately need to unlearn
in order to hop, skip and jump this return
to the place where I sink and you're stern?
Or are we just bang-on banal,
grinding out terms of sale or return
in the room where I sob and you snarl?

The Lammas Rug

The heart's dance is a mite predictable
Carol Rumens

It was a Norfolk harvest:
three saw-blade sunflowers,
a blood-red border, thread-bare leaves:
the rug Great Aunt Ethyl gave Aunt Mary,
who gave it to me, who lent it to you —
who, after a mysterious flood of bilge water
ruined your loo lino, laid my gift on the floorboards,
and when it got swamped in the next sepia spew
refused to clean it, thundering that
maybe *I* had a 'sentimental attachment',
but to *you* it was just an old rug.

…that gave my heart carpet-burn.
An old rug I rolled up, lugged from your flat,
slumped in my arms like a sleeping child,
to the British Library, where I spread it out
on the warm August forecourt, and sat
cross-legged on the ill-scented wool, reading poems,
stubbornly trying not to recall the chorus
of tough, spiky stalks shooting up in your yard.
You'd promised me a sunflower
but here I was dragging my rug back home,
where you couldn't grind your wet heels
into its thin, soiled weave.

O how to heal the root-rot
of an over-watered love? Take my rug
to an autumn altar, light incense with women,
offer apricots and seed bread to the earth?
Buy *1001 Stain Remover* from the hardware shop?
Get down on hands and knees? Will any of that
soak up the dried shadow of whatever it is
that brews between the stories of your flat
seeps out around the cracked base of your toilet
and steeps our growing failure of trust
in the perfume of mould, murk and rust?

The Last Phone Call

You told me to poke holes
in a water bottle lid.

A mate had recommended it:
use a pin, he said.

I had a needle,
but no thimble,

so I rooted in the kitchen
for a hammer,

and tapping very gently
the spiky, shining eye,

pierced the tough green plastic
six or seven times.

Then standing at the window,
the Evian bottle full,

squeezing my new sprinkler
I watered trays of soil —

carefully aiming
the delicate streams,

I felt for a moment
like a goddess of spring rain.

But as the earth darkened
I remembered your shoulders,

how I'd rubbed them
as you cried,

first in my arms
then over the sink

by the ledge where you drowned
those seedlings last summer

not yet knowing
about pins and lids.

Lilith Remembers the Good Times

Some days I hated watching you eat
each sugared almond
that should have been mine.
Some nights I swarmed over your skin,
my body a hot whine of locusts
driving a banquet before it.

Until all that was left was burnt stubble:
your sandpaper cheeks, the shadowy pockets
of a towering flower we'd stripped to a spindle —
my jaws sore, your eyes sucked from their sockets.

Resurrection

                              and when,
                        defying sacred judgement,
                  perfect sense, I'm spoiling in your arms again
                        lips and breasts and wrists
                      grazing in the grasslands of your chest,
                    my Roman nose a small, drugged bee
                        macerating in your armpit's
                            warm Sirocco hymn
                        to carpentry and caraway,
    and when, just as I'm nuzzling   the cinnamon *speculaas*
      the pink puckered flower   your mother used to bring us,
        of your nipple   wild ponies and Pear's soap,
        you softly tell me   wafting smoke, the tang of pee—
      you're seeing a woman in Amsterdam
    who flies over from time to time,
    but you've told her it's not a 'relationship',
    you don't want one of those
    because it hurt you too much when I left,
      and if we're going to have sex   suddenly I'm huddling
        it won't be like before,   on the cold flank of a mountain,
        you won't text me or come visit,   watching from afar
        your music comes first —   a translucent blue sky burst,
                            its wispy, scattered clouds
                        bloat with darkness and backfire
                        into a hopeless summer storm
                            silently besieging
                        the fortress of your ribcage
                      as flocks and herds and hives
                    bleat, bray, screech, low, drone —
                    This isn't love, this isn't love.
                    Go. Stampede. Now. Leave.

The Cruyff Turn

Every advantage has its disadvantage ... and vice versa
                                        Johan Cruyff

A Dutch Renaissance man and a Saskatchewanian Scouser,
we were Ajax v Liverpool v Gospel Oak v Brighton v Regina:
two legendary strikers in mid-life disarray;

a tulip and a maple leaf, sharing bottles of rosé.
Discussing Wimbledon and Wilde, 'post-masculine' aesthetics,
at first we each suspected the other one was gay;

but missing fathers, missing daughters,
our losses flaring like the Furies,
we were hot as chilli chocolate in bed —

though like the vibrating salt and pepper shakers
my brother sent me from Toronto,
when it came to rowing, you swore orange, I saw red.

Chalk and cheese? I disagreed.
But my half-time blackboard game plans
couldn't save us from the mousetrap

of the final penalty shoot-out,
your thumping balls of Gouda ricocheting off our heads
and stopping up the gobs of half the Kop.

Now though I walk alone, limping, bruised, half-blind,
the Cruyff Turn is my mantra:
'Every disadvantage ....' *Hey.*

Advantage Venus. She burned the safety nets
and played us till we dropped in a match too close to call:
The Miracle of Istanbul; Williams S. v Williams V...

And if in love there are no winners,
my North London Netherlander,
remember Total Football, setting tournaments on fire —

your lot torching all the rulebooks, scorching
up the pitch, then sizzling into cinders
beneath a wall of German cleats —

the beauty of the game is never in the score;
silver cups and golden plates
are what a trophy cabinet's for.

Graham's Ninetieth Birthday

Graham was 'feeling numb', he said hoarsely
from his wheelchair, but agreed ninety had a good ring to it
and later raised his voice to say thank you to us all
for our visits, for always bringing him flowers and books.
Trish shone in silver Oxfords, golden giggles;
Grace announced her recent desire to 'perk up' her breasts;
Lee cast gentle aspersions on the notion he was a postmodern poet,
and as Mel passed round her portfolio of sad, Fauvist faces
Paul looked at me across the room, smiled and held my gaze.
There were blue jays in the garden — the first I've ever seen in England —
and goldcrests, with their bright orange caps, flitting between
the wet, fluffy snowflakes whirling outside.
Rhoda spoke about gaining the trust of foxes; Iain recommended
'Six-toed Richardson'; Andrzej asked Chilie for a cup of tea
from the trolley; and I tried to describe
the Graeco-Roman mummy portraits of Fayum: simple, solemn
likenesses, modelled on cypress and sycamore panels,
of people who mostly died young, two thousand years ago.
Graham was born in 1920. He's lived in Greece, Pretoria, Paris,
corresponded with Henry Miller, Dylan Thomas, Ted Hughes,
has paintings in a Swiss gallery of Outsider Art,
and a collection of piercing regrets in his heart. He told me once
he'd call his autobiography *Not Much of a Life*.
Snappy title, I said, and he laughed, like he laughed, finally,
after telling me he spends his days thinking about prisons —
Alcatraz, Strangeways, San Quentin. Graham hates being old:
not being able to walk, or paint; being woken up to take his pills.
Sometimes he says if he could, he'd throw himself out of his window.
Still, I've never asked if he's afraid of death. Sometimes he's afraid
of going out in the car, of being caught short. Sometimes he's happy,
watching the snooker, or EastEnders. He's very fond of Chilie.
Paul and I gave Graham chocolates and a framed Egyptian papyrus,
but what I wish for Graham in his tenth decade is peace,
earthly peace. Forgetfulness of catheters and schedules.
Absorption in the flickering movements of birds and leaves.
A growing friendship with the quiet elation
that can visit anyone, at any time.

Fantasy Football

And if I lay dying
in a clean, white light,
attended by flowers and friends,

would I accept my life then?

Or return the World Cup
brimming with tears,
and twirling an eyeliner moustache

knock back absinthe
from the bottle
to the end?

Plaka (ps)

If sex was the way
we polished the world
until it squeaked and shone,

our embraces were the foam
that dissolved the greasy dirt
leaking from my bones.

Notes

Notes

'Postcard Sent By Someone Else'
zocalo: town square. *hamaca*: hammock.

'The Church…'
Tzotzil: the language of the indigenous people of Chiapas. 'who-peace-bah' is the phonetic pronunciation of the Tzotzil word for beautiful. In Spanish, *hermosa* means 'beautiful'and *sin egal* 'are equal'.

'A Long Eared Tall Tale'
chupacabra: a legendary vampire demon of the South Mexican jungle. *pueblo*: village. *novio*: boyfriend. *periodista*: journalist. *gringa*: female *gringo*. *cenote*: jungle well.

'Sisters of Mercy'
In Hindu mythology, Pampa, daughter of Brahma, performed devotions to Shiva that so pleased the god he married her and took the name Pampapati — Pampa's husband.

In the ancient tradition of Hebrew mysticism, the Kabbalistic tree of life is formed of ten Sephirot, or emanations of G-d:

the formless above

1. Keter

3. Binah   *2. Chochmah*

5. Gevurah   *4. Chesed*

6. Tiferet

8. Hod   *7. Netzach*

9. Yesod

10. Malkuth

Ba'al — Hebrew for 'husband'. IDF: Israeli Defense Forces, which operate a three year conscription period for young men and women. *Muzuzah*: a prayer scroll affirming God's gift of the holy land to the Israelites, attached in a small case to the door frame of Jewish houses.

In 1973 Leonard Cohen performed for IDF troops during the Yom Kippur/Ramadan War. In 2009 he performed in Tel Aviv, despite international protests asking him to boycott Israel, as artists including Elvis Costello and Gil Scott Heron have agreed to do. This time he donated proceeds from the show to create a 'Fund for Reconciliation, Tolerance and Peace,' designed to bring Israeli and Palestinian victims of violence together. As a fan since my teens, I hope his thinking continues to evolve toward solutions that address the underlying injustice that causes the violence in the first place: the Israeli occupation of Palestine.

'Not/A Haibun'
The haibun is a Japanese form that combines haiku with prose. I have fractured this form and blended it with tanka prose, which features the five line tanka, written in syllabic units of 5-7-5-7-7.

al Nakba: 'the catastrophe'. How the Palestinians refer to the creation of Israel in 1948.

'Open Poem to Fred Voss'
A reply to Fred Voss's poem 'Sparkling in Pure Angelic Sunlight' (Ambit 197), which ends with the lines:

> is it bad enough we have to murder
> to live in this world
> why do we also have to make it seem
> so beautiful?

Many poems in Voss's *Hammers and Hearts of the Gods* (Bloodaxe, 2009) explore his complicated feelings about working for the war machine.

'How it happens here'
The names in the last section are those of children who died in the Israel assault on Gaza. The deaths of two of the Hamdan children are documented in *To Shoot An Elephant*, which follows the work of international observers with the paramedics of Gaza, and can be

viewed online. A total of 319 children under the age of 18 appear on the list of 1415 casualties compiled by the Palestinian Centre for Human Rights, including seven teenage militants (of 236 militants in total), and the eleven Nizar Rayyan children referred to in 'Not A/Haibun'. Some of the children were shot in the head at close range. The list may be viewed at www.pchrgaza.org

'Rhetorical Devices'
I am aware that this poem could be seen as inflammatory. I was considering leaving it out of this collection for that reason, but that week a petition arrived in my in-box from the Mamilla Cemetery Campaign. This ancient Palestinian cemetery in Jerusalem is under threat of being bulldozed and replaced by an Israeli 'Museum of Tolerance'. I signed the petition and left the poem in.

'God Save Our Noble Team'
NAFTA is the North American Free Trade Alliance, claimed by many political observers to disadvantage Mexican farmers. Pony-tailed goalkeeper David Seaman famously cried at the exit of England from the 2002 World Cup. Columbian defender Andrés Escobar, known as 'The Gentleman of Football', scored an own goal in the first round of the 1994 World Cup and was shot twelve times outside a bar in Medellín ten days later. The killer shouted 'Goal' when firing each bullet; it is suspected he was a member of a gambling syndicate that had bet heavily on Columbia reaching the second round of the tournament.

'Teutonic Shifts'
'Autonomen': the German Autonome movement was a radical leftist movement focused on squatting and direct action. 'Neubauten': Einsturzende Neubauten, an industrial music group whose name means 'collapsing new buildings'.

'Late Works'
The capitalised phrases are from text-paintings by Derek Jarman. It is possible I have misremembered some, or made the odd one up.

'The Arsonist'
This concrete poem is intended to resemble not only Brighton's West Pier, but also a Tibetan *dorje* (or thunderbolt), a religious artefact used in spiritual ceremonies to banish the non-truth and bring in the truth.

'Peter Crouch'
Though he has since proved (and stretched) his talent, striker Peter Crouch suffered a goal drought at the beginning of his career.

'Lilith Remembers the Good Times'
In the Judaic tradition, Lilith was Adam's first wife. When she claimed equality with her husband and refused to lie beneath him, she was banished to the desert where she gave birth to demons.

'The Cruyff Turn'
Dutch footballer and manager Johan Cruyff [CROWF] was a master of Total Football, a fluid system of playing pioneered by the Netherlands in which players move in and out of position. Total Football revolutionised the game, but did not stop Holland from losing two consecutive World Cup finals, in part due to showing off. Cruyff was also famous for his ability to swivel on the pitch 'like a Parker Knoll chair,' as my fellow Liverpool supporter Paul Lavack once memorably put it.

'The Miracle of Istanbul' refers to the 2005 Champions League Final, in which Liverpool recovered from a 3-0 half time deficit by scoring three goals in six minutes and then beating Milan on penalties. *Yes!*